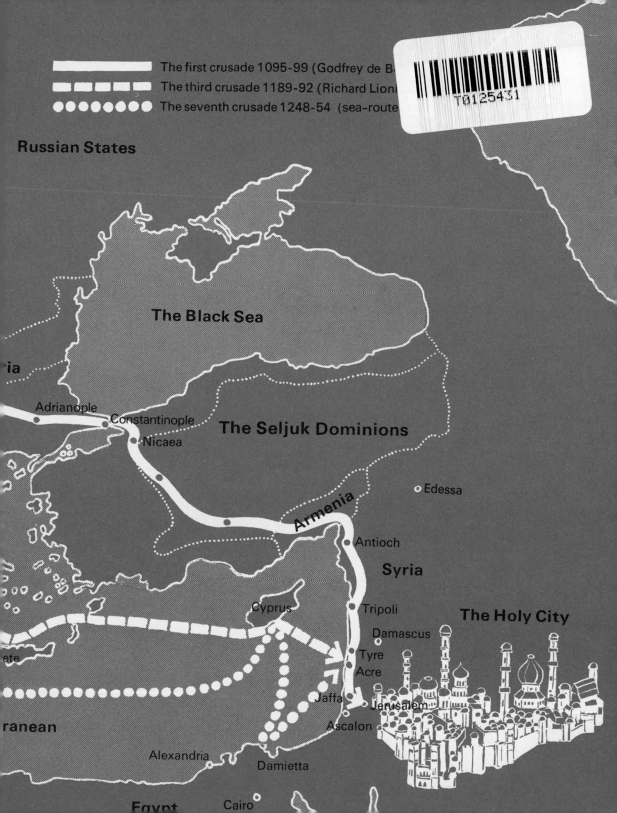

The first crusade 1095-99 (Godfrey de B...

The third crusade 1189-92 (Richard Lion...

The seventh crusade 1248-54 (sea-route...

Russian States

The Black Sea

ia

Adrianople

Constantinople

Nicaea

The Seljuk Dominions

Edessa

Armenia

Antioch

Syria

Cyprus

Tripoli

The Holy City

Damascus

Tyre

Acre

Jaffa

Jerusalem

ete

Ascalon

ranean

Alexandria

Damietta

Egypt

Cairo

Stig Hadenius and Birgit Janrup

How they lived in

the Age of Knights

Translated by Fred Thideman

Illustrated by Ulf Lofgren

Lutterworth Press · Guildford and London

*Over a thousand years ago, in the period which we call
the Dark Ages, the countries of western Europe
were threatened by invading armies from the north and east
as the peoples who had been struggling to make a living
on the sandy flat lands and in the deep forests
of Scandinavia, central Europe, and north Asia,
pushed their way westwards and southwards
in search of new lands and of plunder.
To defend their lands, the leaders of Europe gathered
troops of fighting men who rode into battle
on horseback, armed with lances and swords.
When William, Duke of Normandy, invaded England in 1066,
he led an army of these horsemen, and they rapidly defeated
the Anglo-Saxon foot-soldiers, at the Battle of Hastings.
The defeated Saxons called these warriors 'cnihtas'
(the name which they used for soldiers who were
in the service of a lord or a king) and
the word 'cnihtas' has slowly turned into 'knights'.
At first a knight was simply a warrior who was trained
to fight hard and well in his lord's service.
Presently, however, when the invasions were over,
and life had become a little more settled,
a knight was expected to have new skills and new ideals.
He must still be a brave and loyal warrior, but in addition
he must promise to protect the helpless
and to defend the Christian faith;
he must be well-mannered, truthful and honourable.
For about four hundred years, from the eleventh century
to the fifteenth century, much of a leader's power
depended on the loyalty of his knights,
and the way that a knight lived up to his ideals
could affect the lives of many people.*

'The Age of Knights' sounds like a storybook time,
full of brave knights rescuing beautiful ladies,
but this is not a book re-telling the legends
that have grown up around long-ago heroes.
Instead this book attempts to describe in simple terms
how people lived, seven or eight hundred years ago.

The ruins of many old castles can still be seen today,
but although the strong stone walls and towers have often survived, wooden
roofs, like the ones shown in the picture, usually fell down long ago.

The picture on the left shows a castle in about 1250 A.D.
The castle has steep walls and strong round towers.
Around it is a deep ditch full of water, called a moat,
and across the moat is a drawbridge on iron chains
which are attached to winches inside the gate-house.
If the soldiers on the battlements see enemies coming,
the men in the gate-house can block the gateway
by winching down a steel gate, called a portcullis,
and by winching up the drawbridge
so that no one can get across the moat.

Bodiam Castle in Sussex was built in the late fourteenth century,
and was one of the last moated castles to be built in England.

Beyond the castle gateway, with its steel portcullis,
is a courtyard, and in the courtyard is a well.
Even if enemy soldiers besiege the castle,
the people inside will be able to get water.
The little girl playing by the well is called Anne.
She is nine, and her brother Richard is fourteen.

Children from knightly families, like Richard and Anne,
are usually sent away from home at about eight years old,
to be brought up in the household of another knight or lord.
Richard is being trained for knighthood.
For six years he has served his lord, Sir John, as a page,
and now he has been made squire to his lord's cousin,
a knight called Sir Thomas: he waits on him and
takes care of his weapons and armour; and if ever
Sir Thomas goes to war, Richard will fight at his side.

7

This is Sir John, who is the lord of the castle
and of the countryside around it.

In 1066, William, Duke of Normandy, invaded and
conquered England, and made himself king.
He parcelled out the lands he had conquered,
keeping some for his family, giving some to the Church,
and sharing out the rest among his followers.
Each parcel of land was called a 'fief', and each tenant
'did homage', promising to serve the king loyally.
Onc fief was given to Sir John's great-grandfather,
and this is the fief over which Sir John is now lord.

In return for his fief, each lord promises that
if the king summons him to fight in his army,
he will obey, and will take with him
a stated number of armed knights.
In this way, the king can be sure of having a strong army.

In his turn, the lord parcels out his land to tenant-knights.
Each parcel of land is a 'knight's fee' or 'fief'.
The knight does homage to the lord for his fief
just as the lord does homage to the king.
They both 'owe fealty' to the king:
that is, they must serve him faithfully.

The peasants in each fief must work for the lord.
They must plough the land, sow and harvest the crops,
pay taxes to him, and supply him with milk and
eggs and other foodstuffs.
Some of them are not even free men.

Sir John serves the king faithfully, and with his knights
he goes willingly to war at the king's summons.
In time, however, his descendants decide
to send the king a sum of money, instead of
going to war when he summons them.
The belief that a knight must serve in the king's army
if he is summoned, dies slowly away,
and slowly, very slowly, over the centuries,
the tenants come to think of the land as their own.

Sir John is going on a deer hunt.
The servants blow a shrill fanfare
and Richard sets off at a brisk trot.
The hounds are barking excitedly.
Anne is riding a little way behind the men,
with a party of ladies from the castle.

Anne is glad to be out in the fresh air,
though she would enjoy it still more
if she could ride alongside Richard.
She likes riding better than learning to sew
and weave and embroider,
and to play the lute and to sing.

The hunting party rides through a village, scattering
the pigs and hens who were rootling in the street.
The peasants mostly live on black bread, oatcake and ale,
with a bit of bacon sometimes, or cheese, or an egg.

The peasants can grow grain on their own strips of ground,
but they can only work on their own land
in the time that is left over from working for the lord,
and they can only gather their own crops
when the lord's harvest is safely in his barns.
If the harvest is a bad one
the peasants may starve.

13

Many of the peasants are 'villeins' or 'serfs'.
If the lord sells a piece of land,
he sells the serfs' labour and services with it.
The serfs must work for the new owner
just as they worked for the old one.
They cannot choose which lord they will serve
or what work they will do.

Riding out hawking

When Sir John goes hunting,
he does not always hunt deer.
Sometimes he rides out to hawk instead
with his falcon riding on his wrist.
He lets his falcon fly at wild duck, pheasants, and
other birds, and at rabbits and hares.
The falcon strikes down her quarry with her great talons.

15

After the hunt, Sir John and his followers
come riding back to the castle for a feast.
In the castle kitchens, the cooks are roasting meat
on turnspits, and baking fresh bread.
There is wine to drink, and beer too.

Sir John and his lady sit at the top table in the great hall,
and so does the bishop, their most important guest.
Richard, the other squires, and the pages wait on
the knights and ladies at the tables.
The diners eat with their fingers, and throw bones
and left-overs onto the floor for the dogs.
The knights are dressed as finely as the ladies,
and their clothes are embroidered
with bright silks and gold thread.
Minstrels and jesters entertain the guests.

Anne, who is peeping through the doorway,
would love to take part in the festivities.

Tomorrow, after twelve years of training,
first as a page and then as a squire,
Sir John's eldest son, William, is to be knighted.
That is why Sir John is holding a feast.

All night long William keeps vigil in the chapel,
praying as he kneels in front of the altar
on which his sword is lying.

The next day William takes his vows.
He promises that he will defend the Christian faith,
protect the helpless, and be faithful to his lord.
He is given his armour and his spurs,
his sword-belt and his scabbard.
Then he kneels in front of his father, and Sir John
taps him on the shoulder with his sword.
'I dub thee knight,' he says. 'Arise, Sir William!'
Last of all, William is given
his helmet, his shield, and his lance.

As part of his knightly vows, William has promised
to defend the Christian faith.
Many knights believed that they were fulfilling
this promise, by going on crusade.

Jesus Christ, the founder of the Christian faith, was born
in Bethlehem, in the country called Palestine,
at the eastern end of the Mediterranean Sea.
There he preached to the people, and chose his disciples,
and there, in the city of Jerusalem, in A.D.,33
he was crucified and buried, and, so Christians believe,
rose again from the dead.

Six hundred years later, the Muslim faith
was founded by the preacher and prophet Mohammed,
who was born in the city of Mecca in Arabia,
and who died in the nearby city of Medina in A.D. 632
Like the Christians, the Muslims believed in one God, and
they respected Jesus as a prophet, though they did not
believe that he was the Son of God.

The Christian faith spread through western Europe,
and the Muslim faith spread through much of Asia
and along the coast of Africa to the Atlantic.
There were often raids and battles when the Christians
and the Muslims tried to push one another back,
but as long as the Arabs ruled Palestine, it was usually
possible for Christian pilgrims to travel there
to pray at Jesus's tomb and at other shrines.
But in 1071 the Seljuk Turks over-ran a great stretch
of Asia Minor, and seized control of Palestine and Syria.
The Turks were Muslims too, like the Arabs,
but they were also fierce fighting men.
They closed the shrines, killed the pilgrims, and forced
any Christians they caught to become Muslims, or die.

In 1095 the Pope, as head of the Christian Church, summoned
Christian knights to set out on a great expedition
to drive back the Turks and to seize Jerusalem.
The expedition was called a 'crusade' from a Spanish word,
cruzada, which means 'marked with a cross',
because the Christians took the cross as their badge.
Many knights set out eagerly to fight.

The first crusaders did capture Jerusalem, and set up
small Christian kingdoms on the lands they had conquered,
one at Jerusalem, and others at Edessa, Antioch and Tripoli.
Eighty years later, however, the Muslims re-captured
Jerusalem and most of the land the Christians had seized.
During the next two hundred years, Christian knights
set out on six more crusades.
Many men were killed in the fighting.
Others died of the heat, and of disease.

The only good results of these fierce wars
were the increase in contact between the peoples of Europe
and the increase in Mediterranean trade.

A crusader

Sir John is now going to hold a tournament.
He invites the neighbouring lords to the festivities,
which will last for several days.
Down in the village there is a fair,
and the crowds are entertained by
musicians, singers, dancers and jesters.

A field is cleared and levelled, ready for the
tournament, and a pavilion is built for the ladies.
Anne is allowed to sit there, and she has a fine view
of the 'lists'—that is what the tournament field is called.

Richard is waiting on Sir Thomas.
He has helped Sir Thomas to put on his armour,
and now he hands him the massive lance.

The climax of a tournament is often a melée, which is mock battle between two sides fought out in the lists.

A number of different fighting displays took place
at a tournament, but the most exciting of these, and one
of the most popular, was a joust: this was a special kind
of combat between two warriors, each mounted on a horse
and each armed with a great lance.

William, the newly dubbed knight, takes part in the first
joust of the tournament, which is being held in his honour.
He waits, armed and mounted, at one end of the lists
and his opponent, Sir Giles, waits at the other.
The ladies watch from the pavilion.
A breeze flutters the banners.
Then a trumpet shrills out, to signal the beginning
of the joust; William and Sir Giles lower their lances
and charge at one another down the lists.
As they come within reach of one another, each man
thrusts fiercely with his lance at his opponent
(he is allowed to aim at the shield or the helmet).
The lances strike and shatter, but neither man has fallen.
They gallop on to the end of the lists, rein in
their horses, turn, take fresh lances from their squires,
and are ready to run a second course.

In the fourth course, Sir Giles's lance hits
William's shield full in the centre, and
William reels in the saddle, but manages
to save himself from falling.
In the very next course, William's lance strikes
Sir Giles's helmet, and Sir Giles sways, topples
and thuds to the ground.
Bruised and dizzy, William hears the crowd cheering.

Shield   *Helmet with visor*   *Caparisons*

The jousting goes on for the rest of the day
and all the next day too.
Each knight carries a shield on which his crest is shown.
When he lowers the visor of his helmet, his face
is hidden, but people can still tell who he is
by recognising the crest on his shield.
The horses wear a kind of armour too:
protective coverings made of bright fabric
or leather or, occasionally, metal.
Horse-armours are called 'caparisons' or 'bards'.

The horses thunder down the lists,
the lances thud against the crested shields,
the knights sway in their saddles,
and the crowd cheers, and cheers again, until
at last the trumpets shrill out, signalling that
the tournament is over.
The knights who have fought the hardest and most bravely
are declared to be the champions.
Sir John's wife, Lady Catherine, gives each champion
a wreath of laurel leaves.

28

The ladies and older men watch the melée from the pavilion.

Music-making

In the evening the minstrels sing favourite songs.
First they sing a ballad about King Arthur and his knights,
and then a love song, which, they say,
Tristram wrote to his lady, Queen Isolde,
and then another long ballad telling the story
of a wandering knight and his adventures overseas.

Richard and Anne are listening to the songs.
Perhaps, Anne thinks, when they are both grown up,
musicians will sing a ballad about Sir Richard,
the bravest and most gallant of knights,
and a love song written to the Lady Anne.

First published in Great Britain, 1976
Reprinted 1979

The publishers are grateful to the following for permission to reproduce the photographs used in this book: Bodiam Castle on page 5, Photographic Library, Department of the Environment; photographs on pages 14, 15, 19, 23, 26, 29 and 30 (Additional MS. 42130, ff. 170, 171; Additional MS. 38116, f. 89; Additional MS. 12228, ff. 150v – 151; Royal MS. 2A XXII, f. 220; Royal MS. 2B VII, f. 156v; Royal MS. 20 D VI, f. 54v.), reproduced by permission of the British Library Board

ISBN 0 7188 2200 5
Filmset by Keyspools Limited, Golborne, Lancashire
Printed in Hong Kong

England

London

Poland

France

Paris

Vezelay

Verdun

Metz

Clermont

Vienna

Budapest

The Holy Roman Empire

Venice

Hungary

Belgrade

Genoa

Aigues-Mortes

Marseilles

Pisa

Serbia

Corsica

Rome

The Byza
Empire

Sardinia

Naples

The Norman
Kingdom
of Sicily

THE MOST
IMPORTANT
CRUSADES

Sicily

The M